Student-Led Parent Conferences

by Linda Pierce Picciotto

SCHOLASTIC
PROFESSIONAL BOOKS

NEW YORK • TORONTO • LONDON • AUCKLAND • SYDNEY

Dedication

For my mother, Ellen V. Pierce, and for Janet and Jerry. I thank the students, parents, and staff of South Park School in Victoria, British Columbia, who have made this book possible.

Special Thanks

I want to thank my old friend and former across-the-hall colleague Margaret Reinhard, who has always been ready to try new things and has taught me a lot about teaching. We worked out the first conferences together and never looked back.

I thank Diane Cowden, Shelagh Levey, Wendy Payne, Debbie Marchand, Karen Abel, Vivian Jubb, Linda Travers, Christine Dunsmoor, Larry Layne, Anne Peterson, Carole Miller, and Barbara Leyne for giving me material about their own student-led conferences. You'll see many of their ideas in this book. I also thank Liz Hamblett and Trevor Calkins, present and past principals at South Park, for allowing us the flexibility to work on new evaluation and reporting techniques.

I am fortunate to teach at South Park School in Victoria, British Columbia, where we are encouraged and trusted to follow our own hearts, styles, and interests. Parents are always there to help and offer advice, and students are full of energy and creative ideas. I thank teachers, parents, and students at South Park for giving me important feedback about these conferences.

I would be very happy to hear from teachers who, after reading about our experiences, have tried student-led conferences in their own classrooms. To share information and experiences with colleagues is one of the joys of teaching.

We can learn from each other.

Editor's Note: Although we realize that many children today live in single-parent or other nontraditional settings, to avoid awkwardness we have used the term "parents" throughout, to refer to either parents or other caregivers.

Cover design by Vincent Ceci and Jaime Lucero
Interior design by Carmen Robert Sorvillo
Illustrations by James Graham Hale

Contents

Chapter 1
Why Use Student-Led Conferences? 5

Chapter 2
Looking Back at Our First Student-Led Conferences . . 11

Chapter 3
How the Conference Centers Worked 17

Chapter 4
Discoveries and Responses 29

Chapter 5
Activities at the Centers and Parents' Questions 37

Chapter 6
Other Teachers, Other Schools, Other Schedules 57

Chapter 7
Reports and Comments on Conferences 65

Bibliography
Recommended Reading 72

Appendix
Blank Sample Forms 73

Chapter 1

Why Use Student-Led Conferences?

Why have we so long retained the traditional parent teacher conference format at report card time? After all, the students are left out of the meeting, waiting anxiously for their parents to return home to report what the teacher said about them. Because children are largely left out of the process, they don't learn much from the experience, or gain significant insights about themselves as learners. The teachers are exhausted by hours of talk to parents, often repeating the same things that were written on the report card. Then, too, many parents feel intimidated by private conversations with their children's teacher, perhaps remembering some of their own disappointing school experiences or fearing that their parenting skills may be open for discussion.

Part of the answer lies here: Ideas about education change slowly. If they are comfortable with what they experienced themselves as students, parents often expect to see much the same things at school that they remember from their youth. Parent-teacher conferences have been traditional in schools for a very long time. Some parents may feel shortchanged if these conferences are missing, and may worry that they don't have complete information about their child. And some teachers may think that they are not doing their jobs if they haven't met with parents individually.

Adult conferences are still important, of course, if there are personal, social, or academic issues that need to be discussed frankly without the presence of the child, but these can be held at times that do not conflict with student-led conferences. Both have their place in today's schools. As you read this book, it's important to remember that it's not a matter of choosing one kind of conference over another; each has a valuable role to play in the course of the year. You are the best judge of what will work best for your school community.

What Are Student-Led Conferences?

As the name implies, they are conferences led by the students themselves. Parents come to the conferences to hear about their children's progress.

Through activities and discussions at different "centers" in the room (and sometimes elsewhere in the school, as well) students tell their parents what they have been learning in the different academic, social, physical, and fine arts areas. Children show and discuss both class and individual projects. They may demonstrate skills they are developing in gym and show how they can solve particular math problems. They discuss samples of their written work and read from books they have been enjoying. They show off their artwork. They discuss the areas they wish to work on during the upcoming term. Parents and students may work together to set some goals.

What parents see is an accurate account of their children's growth and development. It is authentic evaluation. Firsthand experience is much more real than any words the teacher can speak or write.

These conferences can be held at traditional report card times or they can be scheduled at other times in the year. The forms students and parents complete at the conferences can become part of the report card for the term or they can be photocopied and sent home as additional evidence of student progress.

Benefits for Parents

Student-led conferences provide a setting for parents to learn more about their children, the school, and the teacher. Being in the classroom with eight other families for an hour one evening is not the same as being there during normal school hours, of course, but the experience does give parents a chance to be with their children in the classroom, to see the materials that are available, to learn some teaching techniques by participating in activities at the different centers, and to see their children interact with the teacher and classmates.

Parents may be happy to see that the atmosphere is much more informal and joyous than it was when they were in school. They can watch their children use manipulative materials to solve fairly sophisticated math problems, and will be pleased to hear children talk with confidence about their own writing or

Eight or more families come to the center at one time.

reading progress, their social development, their science knowledge, and their physical growth. Here are some examples of my students' comments to parents:

— "I can use some 'real letters' if my teacher helps me. Soon I'll be able to do it on my own."

— "I am beginning to leave spaces between my words. I'm going to try to remember to do that. I still mix upper- and lowercase letters in my writing."

— "I am proud of this report on killer whales. Next time I'll put in more details about how they communicate, and I'll spend more time drawing better illustrations and printing more neatly."

— "See, I can figure out how many more 46 is than 27 by using these 10 blocks. First, you put four tens and six ones, then you change one ten for . . ."

Students can also talk about their own behavior and social interactions with more understanding than I used to believe possible:

— "I work better when I am sitting by myself because I like to talk to my friends and other kids bother me."

— "I used to not let people play with me at recess, but now I let anyone play. It makes them happy."

Many parents report that they value the time spent alone with one child at the student-led conferences. Children love the attention, of course, but parents also come to appreciate their child in a new way. They hold conversations that would not have taken place during their normal busy lives. In my experience, parents often come away from these conferences amazed by their own children. Not only are the childeren able to do more than their parents had thought, but they are able to articulate their own progress clearly. Often the students "take charge" of the conference with such confidence that the parents are astonished, for they have not seen that side of their children before. They see the pride their children take in their work and their growth, and they sense

Parents value the one-on-one time with their children.

their children's excitement about learning. Many also see their children show frustration or worry while performing one of the tasks. What parents see at these conferences is authentic. They see their children actually working in the classroom on a series of activities in different areas of study. The learner has been put in the center of the learning and evaluation process.

We know that education is a joint responsibility, shared by school and home. By asking the parents to attend the conferences, to make their own comments on special forms that may become part of the report card, and to work with their children to set goals, we are acknowledging this belief in a tangible way. We teachers cannot possibly give our students as much individual attention as they need to achieve their full potential. By involving parents in such activities as student-led conferences, we can help them become more aware of their children's needs. We can suggest ways they can work with their own child at home, and we can teach them how they can help in different areas by suggesting (at times, demonstrating) enjoyable, productive activities and techniques. The conferences also provide an ideal time to recommend or lend books and materials to families.

Benefits for Students

In the weeks before the conferences, we work with students to prepare for the conferences, and, as a result, students become more aware of their own learning styles, their development, and their areas of strength and weakness. We ask them to select "best work" samples, to think about what they might do to improve in certain areas, and to rehearse what they will say in response to the many questions their parents will ask. The reflection—and the conferences themselves— help students become self-motivated learners, able to set their own learning goals and judge their own work to determine what they need to do to improve.

Hannah, a kindergarten student, demonstrates "hands-on" math to her parents.

Students enjoy the complete attention of their parents for one and a half hours.

Benefits for Teachers

One benefit of student-led conferences for the teacher is not having to lead a series of parent-teacher interviews at each reporting period! Another is the opportunity these conferences provide to see their students in a different light. By listening to the conversations between parents and their children and observing their interactions, teachers can learn if their students are able to explain their accomplishments and articulate their goals. If they can, the class program has prepared them well. If they have trouble, the teacher knows he or she has work to do!

We learn more about our students as individuals as we watch them talk with their parents. We can be more understanding in class after the conferences, and sometimes can adjust programs to meet individual and family needs. It is interesting for teachers to see if parents seem to have positive attitudes toward school, their children, and their progress or if they are critical. We can see if they understand our programs or if we need to do more parent education. By being in the classroom with families we can establish stronger ties with parents. We'll be better able to communicate and work together to make their children's schooling as productive and positive as it can be.

Kieron demonstrates his new code board for his mother and classroom assistant.

Designing the activities for the conferences and deciding which questions to include for parents helps teachers focus on their own practice and programs. What is really important? What activities can I select that will help parents really see what we are doing in class? What questions can we suggest parents ask that will help them learn more about their children?

Can any primary teacher at any school use student-led conferences effectively? I think so. Each teacher will know the school community and will be able to make adjustments to meet the special needs of that group. Teachers are flexible and are experts at taking a kernel of an idea and adapting it to their own needs. I have every hope that this will be the case with student-led conferences.

Chapter 2

Looking Back at Our First Student-Led Conferences

My colleague Marg Reinhard and I had written our report cards in October and were preparing for the first round of parent-teacher interviews. We talked about how tiring these conferences were, although we respected the parents and enjoyed our discussions about their children. The problem, we felt, was the number of talks, one after the other. We both wished that the students could be more involved. It is their schooling we'd be discussing, after all! They should be at the center of the talk, not on the outside. In short, we believed that we could make the conferences an exciting part of our students' educations.

In the classroom we were giving students lots of time to pursue their own ideas and helping them become more aware of their own learning and development. We knew they could talk about their own progress in the different areas of the curriculum—at Author's Circle, during individual conversations, at reading time, during math, after a gym lesson. Why not show off this knowledge to their parents? Why not design conferences that give parents a firsthand look at their children engaged in learning activities?

Trevor Calkins, our principal at the time, was happy to let us try. He asked us to be sure to explain the conferences to our parent group beforehand and to ask for written feedback, which we had planned to do. With his blessing, Marg and I developed a plan.

Planning: The Basics

We came up with a plan that we thought would suit our own programs and school community. It turned out to be so successful that we have changed it very little since. Here's what we set out to do:

1. Incorporate all parts of the curriculum.

Our students would show off their work and discuss their progress in these traditional areas—reading, writing, and arithmetic—of course, but we recognized that school is much more than that. We teachers are trusted to provide experiences and develop abilities in other areas, as well, such as in music, drama, art, physical development, and science. We are also expected to help children develop social skills and to monitor their emotional development.

The centers we chose for our first conferences focused on:
- Intellectual Development: Reading, Writing, Math, and Science
- Aesthetic and Artistic Development: Art and Music
- Physical Development: Gym
- Emotional/Social Development: Short teacher/parent/student conference

We looked for activities that our students could complete successfully, regardless of their levels of development. This meant selecting open-ended activities or presenting a variety from which the children could choose, not just selecting things the least able student could do! We wanted to demonstrate to parents that their children were knowledgeable about their own growth and development.

We wanted to choose activities that would:
- be enjoyable;
- show parents where their child is in his or her development;
- demonstrate how students go about learning in our classrooms.

2. Prepare a schedule.

We decided to ask families to sign up for one of three 1½ hour blocks during the times other classes were holding their traditional parent/teacher conferences. We thought it would be better to have about eight families arrive at one time, rather than schedule families individually. This would take less time, and the general hum of conversations in the room would be good: families wouldn't feel that they were being observed by the teacher. In addition, it would be more pleasant for everyone if there were many families together. Time would not be a factor, either, for each family could take as much or as little time as they needed at each center. In order to accommodate parents who wanted to talk to us privately, we left one block free.

Tuesday: 4:00-5:30

1. _____
2. _____
3. _____
4. _____
5. _____
6. _____
7. _____
8. _____

Tuesday: 6:30-8:00

1. _____
2. _____
3. _____
4. _____
5. _____
6. _____
7. _____
8. _____

Wednesday: 1:00-2:30

1. _____
2. _____
3. _____
4. _____
5. _____
6. _____
7. _____
8. _____

Wednesday: 2:30-4:00

Reserved for parents who wish to have a private talk with the teacher.

Sample schedule

3. Discuss the plan with parents.

On a bimonthly basis, we hold Family Meetings with our parents in private homes. It's probably the best thing we do to foster good communication. These meetings provide good forums for discussing the upcoming conferences.

At the October meeting we each told our parent group of the advantages of the new format and asked for their support. We told them we would ask for their feedback afterward so we could decide what to do at the next reporting period. We assured them that we were still available for parent-teacher interviews if they wished to schedule one. We see many of our students' parents almost every day. Many of them spend a great deal of time in the classroom assisting, observing, and even teaching at times. Because of this, and because of our bimonthly meetings, they have a good idea of our teaching methods and our expectations. They know how their own children are progressing in comparison with other class members. We have a stable population, so many of the parents have been at the school for some time and are a part of our culture.

If this is not the case in your school, you will want to prepare your parents to a greater extent than we found necessary. If you are asking the children to write using invented spelling instead of dictionaries, for instance, you need to talk about your program to parents before the conferences. Explain that this is a beginning phase of writing. Show samples of previous students' work so they know that children will begin to include more letter sounds when they are ready and eventually will shift to more standard spelling and will learn to use dictionaries. If you are not insisting on perfect printing at this stage, explain that, too. In this way you are sure that you are not setting your students up for negative criticism at the conferences.

Consider the other subjects, as well. Is there anything that needs to be explained first to parents? Will they be happy, for example, with your hands-on approach in math? Or will they wonder why the children are not working from textbooks and, perhaps, doing less computation in workbooks or exercise books than they remember from their days in school? Time devoted to explaining your program and expectations will pay off later in smoother conferences and in more enthusiastic, knowledgeable responses to the children's work.

4. Prepare forms for the student-led conference.

We wanted to prepare parents and students for the conferences and provide a place to record parents' comments, so we created a special form that would be useful as a guide at the conferences and could be kept as a record of the event. (See the completed form on page 28.)

We decided that we would encourage families to visit the centers in any order they wished. That would avoid bottlenecks if some centers took longer than others. The one center that had to be visited last was the refreshment center. That would be a reward for a job well done!

5. Make signs to identify each center.

We made signs by folding oaktag. After we wrote the name of the center and added instructions, students decorated the signs, then stood them on tables.

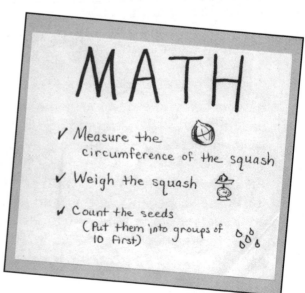

MATH
✔ Measure the circumference of the squash
✔ Weigh the squash
✔ Count the seeds (Put them into groups of 10 first)

6. Prepare parent-feedback questionnaires.

After the conferences, we wanted feedback for ourselves, other teachers, and our principal. Often parents give us helpful information when they write about things from their points of view. In the case of the first conferences, parent response was overwhelmingly positive. (See forms 5 and 6 in the Appendix for questions you might want to ask.)

7. Prepare students for the conferences.

A lot of the preparation work is done during the course of our normal classroom day. The students' main job at the interview is to explain to their parents what they are doing in each area, what progress they have made, and what they are working on. We talk to the students in that way daily when we discuss their work with them.

As the conferences approached, we went over the programs with children and discussed what they would do at each center. As a group we thought of some of the things they could say about their work or activities. We asked them to look through their writing folders and to think about their progress. The math activities were ones children had already enjoyed in class, but I set them up again during class time and helped small groups practice. When we went to the gym during our scheduled time, I told children what they would be doing there during the conferences: They would be explaining their favorite game and demonstrating their favorite activities.

In the weeks before our conferences, students watched and performed many science experiments.

I used the upcoming conferences as a subject for some class writing:

Emily was excited about the conferences:

It will be the sudnt-Led cofrins sone. My
mom and Dad are comeing to it. We are
going to have fun!
i am going to show my mom and dad
arawnd. I am going to rede to my per-
ints. I am going to showtham the caled-
edr jobs to.

Marissa, a beginning writer, was happy, too.

MiMOMCM MABEMiDADLBCM iMGEPRTse
(My mom is coming. Maybe my dad will be coming.
I'm going to read my parents a story.)

Jared reads to his mom.

Dexter and his grandmother share a book at the kindergarten
reading center.

Chapter 3

How the Conference Centers Worked

The first student-led conferences we held included the following centers, which were labeled with signs like this:

Reading
Share books together.
Show what you are learning.

During the week before the conferences, we asked our students to select books that would show their parents what they could read. As this was early in the year and most were not yet independent readers, many chose big books we had read many times together as a class. Some who were already reading selected more difficult material. If the book was long, we asked them to select a few pages or paragraphs they'd like to read aloud. We asked them to think about what they could read now that they hadn't been able to read before. They could talk about that with their parents.

At the center I placed some cards with class members' names on them, for often those are the first words students learn to read. They might surprise their parents by being able to read some of them! It didn't matter if many students chose the same books, for they would not all be at the reading center at the same time.

Stephen was so excited about the conferences that he dressed up!

Jacob explains his writing progress to his parents.

Conference Chats

Mom: What can you read now that you couldn't before?

John: Well, I'm not really a good reader yet. I can read some of my friends' names. I feel like I'm going to start to read soon.

Dad: What books are you reading now?
Sarah: I can read hard books now, chapter books. Not ALL hard books, but some. I can read most of the words in *Charlotte's Web*.

Mom: What do you do when you see words you can't read?
Frank: I sound out letters I recognize the most, and I look at the pictures. Sometimes I just forget it and keep reading, and then I get it later because it makes sense.

We placed a sign like this at the Writing Center:

Writing

Share your writing folders.
What have you learned?
What skills are you working on?
What do you like to write about?

Each student has two collections of writing in the classroom. One is a folder with daily writing. For all at this age, "writing workshop" usually means drawing a picture, then writing one to three sentences about it, using invented spelling. At my almost-daily writing conferences with the students, I write in standard English at the bottom of the page what the child has written.

Sometimes children have to tell me what they have written because the letters they used do not yet correspond with the actual sounds. I talk with the student about the letters and punctuation I use "in standard" and point out how close they were beginning to come to "standard" themselves. My printing is helpful to parents when they try to read their children's work, and it shows them that our goal is to steer our students toward correct spelling and punctuation: Their children aren't going to stay at the "invented" stage forever! They can see evidence of teacher/student conversations on these pages, as well, for I use the margin or back of the page for "teachable moment" lessons.

To compile the second collection, I ask students to write in their special Writing Book once a week. They use the same format as for their daily work. I end up with a bound collection of writing samples that clearly shows children's writing and art development. If I have the student in my class for two or three years the Writing Book is extremely interesting.

It is this weekly Writing Book students show their parents. At the Writing Center, they talk about how their writing is improving, and what stage they are in at the moment in their development. If they have time they can look at the daily writing folder as well, especially if there is something of special interest the student wants to share.

These pages can be selected in the days before the conference by asking students to look through their collections and to mark certain pages with paper clips or stick-on notes. I may ask them to move some of the special ones to their portfolios if I have set up that system in the classroom. Some children want their parents to read every word they have written at school. That takes so long that there isn't enough time for the other centers! A chat about that before the conferences helps. Alert the parents, too. Books and student writing can always be borrowed to complete at home later.

Conference Chats

Mom: Tell me about your writing. What is the difference between your work now and in September?
Allison: Before I didn't leave spaces between my words. I didn't use many letters. Now I leave spaces and I use a lot more correct letters. I use capital letters only at the beginning of sentences and for names. Last year I used capital letters everywhere! I can spell lots of words right.

Dad: What are you working on in your writing?
Pat: I am trying to write longer sentences and I'm trying to use more lowercase letters. I like to write.

Mom: How do you feel about writing?
Ted: I like Writing Workshop. I like to draw the pictures, and then the pictures tell me what to write. I can make real words now. I like sounding them out and writing them down.

This sign indicated the Math Center:

Math

All-day students—
Make a Raisin Bran graph.
Half-day students—
Make an Animal Cracker graph.
All students—
Show your parent(s) what math materials you work with during math activity time.

These math activities showed parents the kinds of things their children were learning and also *how* they were learning, demonstrating "hands-on," some of the methods we were using.

At the time both of us taught K-1 combination classes. We decided to set up different activities for each group. Both the Raisin Bran and Animal Cracker graphs had been part of our math program during the weeks prior to the conferences. We had been working with a variety of graphing techniques with our students. We reviewed these two in order to make sure students still remembered how to do them and could explain them to parents.

These were the instructions we posted at the Math Center:

Raisin Bran Graph

1. Take one scoop (100 ml) of cereal from each of the three brands of Raisin Bran. Put them on the paper towels.
2. Count the raisins in each pile.
3. Complete the graph using three different colors.
4. Ask your parent(s) questions:
   Which brand has the most raisins?
   Which brand has the fewest?
   What differences and similarities do you see when you look at the different kinds of bran cereal? (color, size of flakes, and so forth)
5. Carefully put each brand of cereal back into the correct boxes.
6. Leave the table neat and ready for the next student.

Animal Cracker Graph

1. Place the animals on the graph table, each kind in a separate column.
2. Talk about the results with your parent(s).
   Which animal appears the most?
   How many giraffes are there?
   How many more sheep are there than gorillas?
   Which column has the fewest animals?
3. Place all of the crackers back onto the plate so they will be ready for the next student.

When our students showed their parents the materials they used during math lessons and math activity time, they explained how they used them and which they enjoyed playing with the most.

We have the usual assortment: colored wooden blocks, Unifix cubes, dice, card games, tubs of plastic animals, two-color markers, board games, Cuisinaire rods, base-ten sets, and the like.

Conference Chats

Mom: How do you use these cubes when you do math?

Dave: Linda gives us each some and we use them to help count when we solve problems, like the one about the pigs eating and some go away and some come back.

Dad: What does this graph show?

Mary: It shows that there are more raisins in Post cereal than in the others. See? That line goes up to 23 and that one is 13 and the other one is just 6.

Mom: Which kind of animal appears the most in the animal crackers?

Rachel: The sheep. See, they go way up to the top. There are ten of them. Next is the giraffes. There are five of them. There are two more sheep. I like the gorillas.

In kindergarten, Caelin completes the animal cracker graph for her mom.

Ben and Jamie prepare for the Math Center activity by completing a Raisin Bran graph in class. They'll each repeat it for their parents.

Three years later, Caelin discusses her written work.

At the Science Center, we posted this sign:

Science

Demonstrate and discuss the Magic Milk experiment.

This experiment was a new one for students. In September and October, teachers and students had performed several simple experiments as a class, so they were used to the procedure and the kinds of questions we ask. We thought they'd like a surprise at the conferences. I set up a card with instructions at the Science Center. I used words and drawings so all students would be able to work with a minimum of help from their parents.

Magic Milk (Don't Drink!)

1. Pour milk into the bowl. Fill it up to the black line.
2. Pour a thimbleful of liquid detergent into the center of the milk.
3. Add two drops of food color.
4. Discuss the experiment with your parents.
   What did you see?
   Why do you think that happened?
   Can you think of another experiment you might do with the milk and detergent?

Mom: Wow. Why do you think it started swirling around like that?
Sam: Maybe the milk and soap don't mix so they just sort of chase around. The colors show how it's moving.

Dad: What other experiment could you do with these materials?
Alicia: We could put the detergent in first and then add the milk. Then we could put it in a tall, skinny bottle to see what happens.

Art

Show and discuss the artwork that you have displayed in the room.

I made sure that each student had chosen at least two works of art for display in the room or in the hall. The students and I talked about the kinds of things they might say to their parents about the art. I suggested that they also make positive comments about the work of some of their classmates to show how we all appreciate the efforts of others.

Conference Chats

Dad: Which picture do you like best?
Steven: I like the one of the corn plant. I like the way I outlined first and then colored in.

Mom: Tell me about your picture.
Meg: It's a storm. I drew it after Linda read a couple of poems about storms. I like the way I made it look like the wind is blowing.
Mom: Yes, the trees are bending over and the watercolor wash you used makes it look rainy. It looks like a real artist made that picture.
Meg: I *am* an artist.

This sign was posted at the Gym Center:

Gym

In the gym tell your parent(s) how to play your favorite game, or demonstrate your favorite activity.

Before the conferences we talked about games we had learned. Students decided which ones they might show their parents. I asked them what equipment they would like me to put out so they could demonstrate favorite activities. As a result of our conversation I put out jump ropes, balls, hoops, a balance beam, and beanbags.

Conference Chats

Dad: What is your favorite activity in the gym?

Len: I like to play with the balls. I can dribble the ball better than last year, and sometimes I can make a basket.

Dad: I see that you're getting really good. Great! What are you working on now?

Len: I can't really skip rope that well. I want to play more floor hockey.

Mom: Tell me about your favorite game.

Amanda: It's Beanbag Tag. Everyone has a beanbag on their head and walks around, and when it falls off you stand there and someone comes along and picks it up for you. I like to play with the parachute, too, but it's not really a game.

We placed this sign at a table where we would confer with each family.

Conference Table

Have a Talk with the Teacher Here.

Meeting parents and children at this conference table gave me a chance to say a few positive things about each student, to comment on behavior, to help set some goals or begin to solve some problems. I took notes so I wouldn't forget the questions parents asked or the steps I promised to take to help certain children, such as making referrals to the speech therapist or changing someone's seat at carpet time!

However, I began to find these conversations a bit awkward. Some parents really didn't know what to ask, some students seemed ill at ease, and meanwhile, a log-jam of families began to back up, waiting patiently for their turns with the teacher. Since serious behavior or academic concerns had been addressed by personal contact earlier in the year, I wondered: Was this particular center necessary?

I decided it was not, and at subsequent conferences, I found it was better to circulate while the families were at the centers, joining different groups from time to time to give mini-lessons, point out progress that a certain child had made, and suggest or demonstrate ways parents could help at home. I could also make sure that things were operating smoothly, and if I noticed that families were having a little difficulty, I could quietly intervene to set things in motion again. Whether you decide to use the conference table or circulate freely, give yourself permission to change whatever doesn't work in favor of what does, or what suits your teaching style best.

Conference Chats

Parent: No one is at the Science Center. Let's go there now.
Student: No, I want to go to them in order; math is next.
Teacher: Molly, your parents will really enjoy looking at the science experiment. Take them there and then go to the Math Center afterward.
Student: Okay.

Parent: Brenda, what's that word? Sound it out. No, it's not *gone*. Don't you see that there is no *n* in it? It's *go*. What's the next word?

Teacher: May I show you how you can read with Brenda in a way that will be more fun for both of you? [demonstrates choral reading, leaving out words occasionally that Brenda is able to fill in by context] Brenda can't really "sound out" yet—she doesn't know all her letter sounds.

Parent: I see. You do it so it sort of flows along.

Teacher: Yes, just have fun together. At school, we use phonics and many other methods to learn reading. She'll begin to read when they all come together for her. At home, just enjoy books!

Refreshment Table
When you are finished, serve your parent(s) juice and cookies, and enjoy some yourself!

This was an important part of the evening for our students! Children had made muffins as a part of our cooking program in the weeks before. (We then froze the treats and thawed them right before the conference.) To stress the importance of good nutrition, I added orange slices to the table. A tablecloth and a bouquet of flowers made the table attractive.

STUDENT-LED CONFERENCES
Linda Picciotto and Marg Reinhard
November 28--4:00-5:30 or 6:30-8:00
November 30--1:00-2:30

Student name ___Rachel___ Parent(s) ___Ed___

Please go to each of the following centres during your visit to discuss each area of your schooling with your parent or parents. You may visit the centres in any order.

CENTRES	PARENT COMMENTS
✓ **Reading** Share books together. Show what you are learning.	Rachel enjoys books and is beginning to recognize a few words.
✓ **Writing** Share your writing folders. What have you learned? What are you working on? What do you like to write about?	What interesting stories! We love the pictures. Her writing has really changed since Sept. - lots of real letters.
✓ **Math** All-day students: Make a "raisin bran graph" Half-day students: Make an "animal cracker graph" All students: Show your parents(s) what math materials you work work during math activity time.	Rachel did a good job of explaining the graph to us. She likes math, she says. Great!
✓ **Science** Demonstrate and discuss the Magic Milk experiment	Fun- we'll try more experiments at home.
✓ **Art** Show and discuss your art work that is displayed in the room.	Wonderful paintings. We liked that clay pot, too.
✓ **Gym** In the gym tell your parents how to play your favorite game. Demonstrate your favorite activity.	Rachel has learned to skip rope! She loves to play salmon & trout.
✓ **Have a talk with the teacher at the conference table.**	Thanks!
✓ **When you have finished, serve your parent(s) juice and cookies, and enjoy some yourself!**	Delicious. A nice way to end.

This form for parents serves as a guide to the learning centers.

Chapter 4

Discoveries and Responses

The first conferences went well. In fact, they were even more successful than we ever imagined. Our prediction that these conferences would be a lot less tiring and much more beneficial than the traditional parent-teacher interviews was proved correct. Most parents agreed, and certainly the children were proud and happy. We actually looked forward to the next round and, almost immediately, began to think of activities we'd prepare for the next centers.

We hadn't realized how important the conferences would be to the students. Some dressed up for the occasion. All seemed to love being the center of attention for the hour and a half. It isn't often that they have the full attention of a parent—sometimes *both!* We were happy that we had asked families to leave siblings at home, for some brothers and sisters who did turn up were indeed a distraction for the parents and for other families in the room. We found that we had a perfect opportunity to join "conferences in progress" to make observations, note progress in certain subjects, talk about attitudes and work habits, and suggest ways parents could support their children at home. Comments made during that time—right when the subject was being discussed by the families—made so much more sense than if they had only been written on a report card.

The conferences also gave us opportunities to give mini-lessons to the students, with the parents looking on. We could gently show parents better ways to read with their children, for instance, if we saw that a child was being asked to "sound out" every word he or she couldn't read. We could also show parents how to give their children "thinking time" when they were trying to solve a math problem instead of *telling* them how to go about solving it. We could model positive, encouraging remarks that give children self-confidence. We feel that these suggestions are appreciated more, and perhaps received with more openness when they are made in the context of the conferences. Sometimes the printed word seems a bit harsh, and words are often misinterpreted. Parenting is not easy, and everyone is sensitive to criticism. When sug-

29

gestions are made in person, and with the children present, parents can see that they are made in the right spirit, and that we're all trying to do the best we can for their children.

Learning In Advance

We also realized that taking part with us (to some extent) in *preparing* for the conferences had been valuable for the students in many ways. It increased knowledge, built self-esteem and self-confidence, made children more aware of their own learning and development, and helped them realize that all areas of the curriculum are important.

Taking part in the preparations helped the children become more aware of *why* we do what we do at school. How do we decide what is important? How can we organize the portfolios so they will be easy to use? How they will explain their work to their parents? How will we decide which pieces of work to select? We saw that the process helped them focus on their own abilities and progress.

Parent Responses

After the first conferences we sent home questionnaires to parents so we could gather their reactions. Were they as pleased as we had been with the results? They were. Only one parent suggested that he would rather have had a teacher-parent interview. We talked to him and arranged for a private talk. He agreed that having *both* the student-led conference and the parent-teacher conference gave him a much more complete picture than the parent-teacher talk would have alone.

Others overwhelmingly preferred the new format and wanted them to continue. Here are some examples of the responses we received from our parents:

➤ I liked seeing/feeling my child showing, demonstrating, and guiding facets of her learning. She appreciated being in charge of her environment and learning.

➤ I know that my own thoughts about my daughter will change as she grows up. It will be interesting in later years to read my own remarks about her at this stage of her development! Thanks for giving me the opportunity to do this.

☛ *I felt the conference was useful and informative. I appreciated the students being included in the process. It was completely nonthreatening for them, unlike waiting for Mom and Dad to come home and "report."*

☛ *Frank was very nervous, but I'd like to see it continue. Maybe next time he'll be able to cope better.*

☛ *The conferences gave us a special time alone without siblings. I felt a strong connection to Jeb's learning. I was impressed by the amount of self-reflection he had done, his pride in himself, his joy in sharing his world with us.*

☛ *I liked seeing and talking about activities and accomplishments. Carlos does not talk much about what goes on in class.*

One teacher sent this questionnaire home after a conference:

1. Did your child enjoy being part of the conference?
2. Did you feel the time was well spent and valuable?
3. Were your concerns addressed?
4. What was the most valuable part of the conference for you?
5. What was the least valuable part of the conference for you?
6. If goal-setting was discussed, do you feel it was realistic?
7. Any other comments?

Forms 5 and 6 in the Appendix show ways you may gather feedback from parents.

Concerns and Solutions

Although we all like to read positive comments, sometimes the most useful responses from parents and students are those that express concerns or talk about problems they experienced.

- **Concern:** *The conference took too long. Robert got very tired and was unresponsive and distracted at the end.*

- **Solution:** Some centers could be optional. Alternatively, we ask families to visit what we consider the most important centers first, making it clear that there is no set time for each center but that none should take more than 15 minutes. Perhaps this family could consider coming to an afternoon session instead of an evening one. When we prepare our students, we should ask them to select short passages of reasonable length for read-alouds and to choose only some of their writing to share. One parent complained that her child read for a half hour, so little time was left for the other activities!

- **Concern:** *It would have been helpful to have more information about what was expected from parents.*

- **Solution:** In addition to the parents meetings before the conferences, we plan to write instructions to hand out at the conferences or to send home shortly before the conferences. We will emphasize that children can go to the centers in any order and that there is no set time for any one center. We need to remind parents that their child is in charge and that it is the parents' job to write their own brief remarks on the form and to write a quote from their child, as well. It might be useful to prepare a list of sample remarks, so they know that their comments can be quite short and simple.

- **Concern:** *I found it distracting to have to write my comments at the conference.*

- **Solution:** We could suggest that parents take the forms home to write their comments. I would urge them to write their children's remarks at the conference itself. I suspect that parents would hear lots of "I don't know, I forget" answers in response to questions that they ask later. Maybe parents think that their comments have to be detailed and brilliant! We need to let them know that simple phrases are fine.

- **Concern:** My child was embarrassed at the Music Center. He didn't want to sing out loud.

- **Solution:** We could make the Music Center optional, or we could put it in a different room with a Do Not Disturb sign on the door. Or we could select activities like clapping to a beat, discussing favorite songs, or talking about composers or musical instruments.

- **Concern:** My child was nervous.

- **Solution:** Be sure the children are well prepared. Some will still be jittery, but they will be able to get through it and will be proud of themselves for having risen to the challenge!

Student Responses

At school we asked our students to write about their experiences at the conferences. The form I used had a place for a picture and open-ended sentences for students to complete. Some student responses follow.

Another teacher used the form below, with lines provided for the student's response after each sentence beginning.

1. My parent was _____

_____

2. I felt good _____

_____

3. I was disappointed that _____

_____

4. I wish _____

_____

Student response samples

Name joey

Date Nov. 9 1995

Our Student-Led Conferences were held this week. Mine was on **tuesday**. My **dad** came to my conference.

My favourite centre was **Books**

My **dad** said **that he likd my art wrlk.**

I **likd relding to my dad.**

Student response sample

Special Situations

- **Situation:** *What happens when a child's parents are not living together?*

- **Suggestion:** If their relationship allows (or at least they are in agreement about the needs of their child), they can attend the conferences together. If they do not want to visit on the same evening, each can sign up for a different day. Their child is usually very happy to take each through the centers separately. Encourage each parent to contribute comments to the form.

- **Situation:** *What if the parents do not speak English?*

- **Suggestion:** If the parents feel comfortable about coming to the school, their child can conduct the interview in the language they speak at home. If this is not possible, perhaps the school could organize a translator service for such occasions, or their child could take the necessary material home for a home conference.

- **Situation:** *What if the parents will not come to the conferences?*

- **Suggestion:** We have found that this is rarely a problem. The children will usually insist that they come! However, it does happen. Perhaps the student's older "buddy" can attend the conference, or the custodian, the principal, the secretary, or an assistant the child knows. Maybe an aunt, uncle, grandparent, or family friend will visit.

- **Situation:** *What happens when parents are critical of your program or ask questions that you find difficult to answer because of time limitations?*

- **Suggestion:** Arrange a time for them to talk to you when their child is not present, and ask them to continue with the rest of the conference. Be sure that you have explained at the beginning of the year that you will be happy to talk to them about any concerns.

- **Situation:** *What if parents have more than one child in the school?*

- **Suggestion:** Parents handle this in different ways. Sometimes one parent will attend one child's conference while the other attends the other's. Sometimes they change places at the halfway point. Sometimes they spend just 45 minutes in each room. They can also choose to sign up for two different time periods in order to spend the full amount of time with each child.

Chapter 5

Activities at the Centers and Parents' Questions

You will want the activities at each center to reflect your own classroom program. This chapter contains activities that I have found successful over the years as well as activities other teachers at different primary grade levels have chosen. They may help you as you design your own program.

You do not have to include each center at each conference. If you have done a lot in science one term, for instance, you may want to emphasize that and leave out social studies, or include a computer activity. If you've been teaching library skills, one of your centers could be in the library. ("Show how you can use the card catalog [or computer] to find *Learning About Wolves*.")

You may set up many centers, designating certain ones as *must* be done and others as *may* be done, if time permits. Ask students to choose one or two activities among several listed at a certain center. That would cut down the amount of time required, allow children to choose activities they are comfortable with, and show parents the wide range of classroom learning experiences you provide.

Helping Parents Ask Good Questions

When you have decided which centers you want, list questions parents can ask their children. This will make the conferences run smoothly and be as meaningful, helpful, and successful as possible.

Formulating good questions is an art. Parents may not know how to ask questions that will help their children explain clearly their work, activities, growth, and plans. Good questions will lead to interesting conversations and will let parents know what we teachers are looking for when we evaluate students.

Tips:

• Design conferences of reasonable length. When children become tired, the conferences deteriorate quickly!

• Some teachers write detailed instructions for center activities and some write simple, general suggestions. Do whatever suits your style, the needs of your school community, and the purpose of the conferences. If you would like parents to note certain skills or learning styles, set up activities that will demonstrate those. Here is an opportunity to do some authentic evaluation.

• It is so tempting to include many different activities because you want your students to show off all they know and all you are teaching! When you have completed your list, ask a parent or another teacher to look over your plan. They'll tell you if they think you've included too much. Strive for brevity, simplicity, and clarity!

• If activities and questions are well designed, parents and teachers alike learn a great deal about the children—and children can learn about themselves, as well!

Center Activities and Questions for Parents to Ask

Some questions that are very general deal with students' attitudes or interests. Others are specific to special studies. The questions can be printed on the program form or can be written on cards or charts at the centers. (See samples throughout this section.)

On the next few pages, you'll see examples of Suggested Activities and Suggested Questions for parents to ask for each area. Choose from two to four questions for your Suggested Questions list in each area. Some parents feel that they must answer every question and complete every activity, so be careful about what you ask!

These sample questions are from different teachers at different primary grade levels at different times of the year. As with your center activities, questions will depend on your own teaching style, your students, their parents, the time of year, the current focus in your classroom, and time limitations.

Reading: Suggested Activities

- Show a book by one of your favorite authors. Tell why you like that author.
- Read to your parents the material you have selected for this conference.
- Read from the book you choose to show how well you can read now.
- Show two or three of the books you especially enjoyed listening to.
- Tell about your favorite kind of reading—fact, fiction, fairy tales, magazines, and so on.
- Explain SQRT time and shared reading time.
- Read a book or part of a story to your parent(s).
- Show your story map of *The Mare's Egg*. Retell the story. Explain how we set criteria before mapping and then evaluated our work when it was completed.
- Show your project on *The Borrowers* and explain how it works.
- Show and read the page you made in the big book about puddles.

READING

Activity

Share books together. What books do you like to read or listen to?

Suggested questions

Is there anything you can read now that you couldn't before?
Show me some of your favorite books.

Student

"I like to read."

Parent Thomas loves to "read" books. He can even really read a few words!

READING

Activity

Read to your parents the material you have chosen.

Suggested questions

What can you read now that you couldn't before? What can you do when you can't read a word?

Student

"I can read chapter books now. I like mysteries."

Parent We're very pleased with Mary's progress. She reads with expression.

Reading: Suggested Questions

- Tell me about your reading. Is there something you can read now that you couldn't read before?
- What do you do to try to read words you don't know right away?
- Which books do you look at or read during reading time?
- How has the home-reading program helped you to become a better reader?
- What are your favorite kinds of reading material? (picture books, chapter books, poems, magazines, comic books)
- Do you read at home?
- How do you feel about reading?
- What would you like to read next?

A student shares her book summary with her mother.

Kevin shows his dad his sketchbook.

"My writing is getting better, and I write so much!"

Writing: Suggested Activities

- Read aloud three pieces you've selected that show different kinds of writing.
- Read your published story.
- Print your name on the chalkboard. What can you do now that you couldn't do in September?
- Share your writing folders and your writing book. Tell what you are learning about writing. Look at your Writing Self-Evaluation sheet together.
- Read the two selections from your journal that you selected for your portfolio.
- Spelling:
    - Show the list of words that you know how to spell.
    - Make a word family for *may* or *tried*.
    - Print your name with letters of the correct size.
    - Show your parents your Spelling Guide. Tell how you use it when you proofread your work.
- Compare a piece of writing from September with a piece from November. How has it changed? What are you pleased with? What would you like to do differently?
- Show the note taking (webbing) you and your partner did on one of the animal books.
- Show your draft copy and final version of the story you wrote about your pet. Show what things you changed when you edited and proof-read your draft.

WRITING
Activity

Look at your writing collections with your parents. Compare your fairy tale draft with the final copy.

Suggested questions

What skills are you working on now?

What kind of writing do you like best?

Student "I love to write. I am writing a long story. I use more colorful language".

Parent

Great writing and her spelling is much better now.

WRITING
Activity
Share your writing folders with your parent(s). On the "writing development chart" show where you are now.

Suggested questions
What skills are you working on now?
What are you trying to remember to do when you write?
Show me your best writing.

Student
"I'm getting better at writing. I use some real letters."

Parent I'm impressed by how aware Thomas is of his own progress! It's coming!

Writing: Suggested Questions

- Tell me about your writing. What are you doing now that you couldn't do before? (longer sentences, descriptive writing, spelling, use of punctuation, writing poems)
- What do you like to write about?
- What do you like best about Writing Workshop?
- Do you do any writing at home?
- What skills are you working on to become a better writer? (spacing between words, using upper- and lowercase letters, using standard spelling more, writing longer stories, using punctuation)
- Are you able to do cursive writing easily now?
- What piece of writing are you most proud of?
- What is your favorite Writing Workshop page?

Math: Suggested Activities

- Measure your hand and your parent's hand. Record data on the sheet.
- Measure your leg and your arm. Which is longer? Record your answer.

- *Computer:*
  - Draw a large egg. Make lines or designs across it.
    Use the paint can to fill the empty spaces with patterns.
- Build one of the following numbers using Diene's blocks and place-value mats: 64, 523, and 6794. If you know how, show it in expanded form and standard form using the colored cards.
- At the Mass Table complete the Guess and Check chart. How many grams do you think each rock weighs?
- Choose two of the following four activities:
  1. Play either The Trading Game or Scoop It to show how you can count with money.
  2. Have a game of Equation Dice Toss.
  3. Do some of the Hundreds-Day activities and play one math game.
  4. Build a model of, then solve, one of the following addition questions.
     Use the place-value mat and the bean banks.

No regrouping		Regrouping
26	317	458
+53	+452	+236

- Show the materials you like to work with at math time.
- Teach your parents how to play the card game Ninety-Nine. (Parents: Take the rules home for future games.)

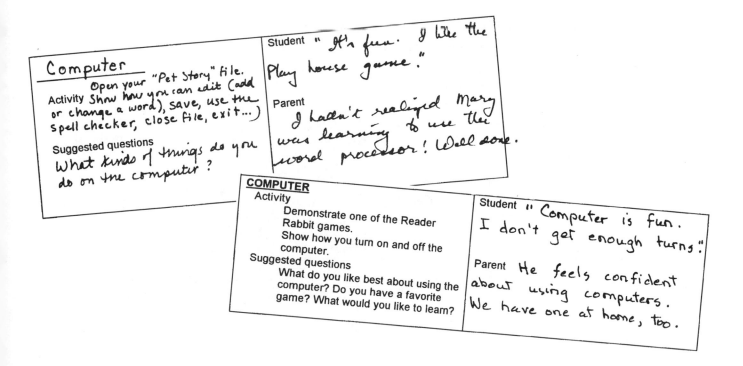

Computer
Activity Open your "Pet Story" file. Show how you can edit (add or change a word), save, use the spell checker, close file, exit...)

Suggested questions
What kinds of things do you do on the computer?

Student " It's fun. I like the Play house game."

Parent I hadn't realized Mary was learning to use the word processor! Well done.

COMPUTER
Activity
Demonstrate one of the Reader Rabbit games.
Show how you turn on and off the computer.
Suggested questions
What do you like best about using the computer? Do you have a favorite game? What would you like to learn?

Student " Computer is fun. I don't get enough turns."

Parent He feels confident about using computers. We have one at home, too.

MATH

Activity

Measure the circumference of the pumpkin: **43 cm**

Weigh it **3 k**

Count the seeds in the dish **35**

Show your parent(s) what math materials you work at math time.

Suggested questions

What can you do now that you couldn't before? Is there something you would like me to help you with at home?

Student " *It's fun to weigh and count.* "

Parent *Skills are developing. Fun activities!*

MATH

Activity *Take your parents to the 2 math centres, coins and probability cartons.*

Suggested questions *What can you do with numbers that you couldn't do earlier this year? Is there anything you should be working on at home?*

Student " *I like to make graphs and play math games. I'm getting better at regrouping. I want to learn my times tables.* "

Parent *We're glad Mary likes math, seems to understand well. Loved the probability exercise!*

- Complete a "fastener" graph for you and your parents, using the form at the table. What is holding your clothes together? (zippers, snaps, hook and eyes, Velcro, buttons, snaps)
- Take your parents to the two math centers, Coins and Probability Cartons. You will find instructions there.
  1. Show six ways to write 14.
  2. Use the beans to solve 57+18.
  3. Use the junk boxes to make a number story.
  4. A problem to solve:
     In the woods there are 12 owls. Six of them are great horned owls and the rest are screech owls. How many screech owls are there?

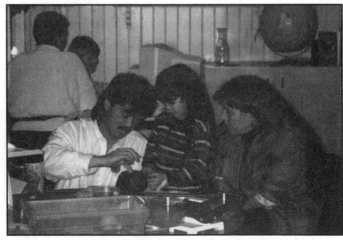

Satomi demonstrates how she can weigh the squash at the Math Center.

Sara teaches her mom the "bean trading" game.

Chris demonstrates how to measure the circumference of a pumpkin.

Math: Suggested Questions

- Can you do something now with numbers that you couldn't do before?
- Is there something you wish you could do better?
- Do you enjoy playing math games?
- Which class card game can you play most easily?
- Which math activities do you enjoy the most?
- What more would you like to learn about mathematics? (working with numbers, graphing, patterns, measuring, weighing, estimating, problem solving)
- What can you practice at home?
- Is there anything we can do to help you?

Science: Suggested Activities

- Demonstrate the Blast-Off experiment. How does the balloon make the rocket shoot along the string?
- Show your science notebook. Which experiment did you enjoy the most?
- Look at your Cooking Book. What was your favorite recipe? Why?

- Follow directions carefully as you demonstrate the Floating Drops experiment. Wear the lab coat, if you wish.
- In the Dinosaur Study Lab, show what you have been learning about dinosaurs. Tell which is your favorite dinosaur. Why do you find it interesting?
- Show the Animal Group poster. Look at the cooperative learning chart and explain what your role was. Show your parent(s) the cocoon that was spun before our very eyes.

Dylan explains that salmon lay their eggs deep under the ground.

- Show your parents your Tree Book. Tell three things you learned about Wildlife Trees at our visit to Francis King Park. Look at the leaves closely under the magnifying glass.
- Take your parents on a tour of our Salmon Murals. Tell how each mural shows a stage in the salmon's life. Which mural did you work on? Now read your own salmon booklet together. Which is your best illustration? Using the class drawing as a guide, tell what you remember about the fish that the naturalist cut open for us at the river.
- Discuss your Egg Incubation Book with your parents.
- Look through your science notebooks and discuss the projects we have been working on. Look at the salmon in the aquarium.

SCIENCE

Activity

In the "Dinosaur Lab", show what you have been learning about dinosaurs.

Suggested questions

What is the most interesting thing you learned in your study? How do scientists know how old the bones are? Which is your favourite dinosaur?

Student

" They check the age of the rocks where they found the bones."

Parent

I think we have a future scientist A...

SCIENCE

Activity

Do the "Magic Candle" experiment at the science centre. Show your science notebook.

Suggested questions

Why do you think the water rose in the jar? Which "write-up" is your best?

Student " I liked my own experiment best but I did a good job writing up Amanda's "Layers" experiment."

Parent

We're so pleased to see Mary doing and recording experiments.

Science: Suggested Questions

- What are some of the interesting things you learned in science?
- What have you enjoyed learning/studying the most?
- Which experiment, besides your own, did you find most interesting? What did you wonder when you watched it?
- Which write-up shows your best work?
- What did you like best about the science experiments? (watching, discussing, performing, drawing, the write-up)
- Which part of the salmon study did you find more interesting?

SCIENCE NOTEBOOK   date 11/25

* Dry Paper
Name of experiment

* Allison Louisa Witter
Name of scientist

1. I scrunched up a peice of paper and put it in to a glass
2. I filled up a bukit with water
3. I turnd the glass up side down and lowered it into the water.
4. I took the glass out and The paper was dry.

Aidan tells his mom what he learned about beavers.

Tristan and his parents discuss his science notebook.

47

Social Studies: Suggested Activities

- Show your parents how the post office operates. You will need a piece of paper, two tokens and a name from the basket. Print a letter, address the envelope, and mail the letter. To whom did you write your letter?
- Show your parents the clinic, the nurse's desk, and the waiting room. Show your parents your patient chart.
- Show your parents the giant map of Canada we made together. Tell which province you completed and who your partner was. What part did you do?
- Show your papier-mâché map. Is it accurate? Compare it with the map on the wall.
- Show your research book about the province you studied.
- Look at the class map of Tom Thumb Safety Village. Using one of the little cars, tell about three different safety rules for cars. Using one of the plastic people, tell about three different safety rules for pedestrians.

Music: Suggested Activities

- Visit Marne's* music center. Use the hand signs you use when you sing "Good-bye, Marne." Clap the rhythm written on the chart. Sing part of "Food, Glorious Food," a song from our production of *Oliver*.
- Sing the song and explain the game *Doggy, Doggy, Where's My Bone?*
- Clap the rhythm on the chart and sing the song, using hand signs for Sol and Mi.
- Go through your music booklet "My Own Song Book" together. Tell which is your favorite song.

* Marne is our music teacher. We asked her to design a center that would show parents what their children are learning in music lessons.

MUSIC

Activity

At the music center, show the hand signs for the "Good-bye, Marne" song. Clap the rhythm. Explain how to play, "Doggie, Doggie, Where's My Bone?"

Suggested questions

What do you do in music class?
Did you join the primary choir? (Why or why not?)
Do you have a favorite song?

Student "I like music lessons and I like to sing in class with the guitar."

Parent I'm glad Thomas is in choir. He sings a lot at home.

MUSIC

Activity

Visit Marne's centre and follow instructions there.

Suggested questions

What are you learning in music class? Why did you choose (or not choose) to be in primary choir?

Student "I like music. It's very, very fun."

Parent Mary enjoys music of all sorts.

Music: Suggested Questions

- What have you been learning in music class?
- Why did you choose (or not choose) to be in the Primary Choir?
- Do you have a favorite song?
- What do you remember most about our school production of *Oliver*?
- Which musical activities did you enjoy most this year? [Teacher might list them here.]
- How has your ability in music, or your understanding of music, or your enjoyment of music, grown this year?

Noah claps a rhythm for his mom at the Music Center.

Art: Suggested Activities

- Show your artwork. Tell how you feel about it. Which is your favorite piece? What would you like to create next?
- Use the paper provided at the center. Draw a picture of yourself. Have your guest(s) draw themselves.
- At the art center show what you know about primary, secondary, and complementary colors.
- Tell what you remember about one exhibit you saw at the Art Gallery. (forest mural, Korean folk art, snow scenes, lion rugs)
- Show your Continuous Line Drawing with a Wash. Explain the criteria you had to follow. Tell why you chose to display it.
- Show and talk about your artwork displayed in the classroom or the hall. Which picture do you like the most? What do you like about it? Which art activities do you most often choose to do? (painting, drawing, cutting and pasting, building with clay, wood, art box materials, and so on)
- Show your black-and-white nature drawing.
- Find the prints of paintings by Vincent Van Gogh and Robert Bateman. Point out the important features.
- Show your oil pastel drawing based on the style of Ted Harrison. How is your work like Mr. Harrison's? How is it different?
- Choose pictures you've made to explain realistic, abstract, and surrealistic styles.
- Show your papier-mâché alien and explain the steps involved in making it.

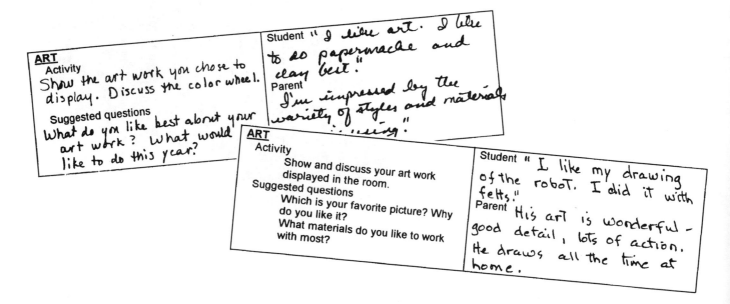

ART
Activity
Show the art work you chose to display. Discuss the color wheel.
Suggested questions
What do you like best about your art work? What would like to do this year?

Student "I like art. I like to so papermache and clay best."
Parent
I'm impressed by the variety of styles and materials ......"

ART
Activity
Show and discuss your art work displayed in the room.
Suggested questions
Which is your favorite picture? Why do you like it?
What materials do you like to work with most?

Student " I like my drawing of the robot. I did it with felts."
Parent His art is wonderful — good detail, lots of action. He draws all the time at home.

Alex talks about the art in his portfolio.

Hannah shows her mom how she mixes secondary colors.

Art: Suggested Questions

- Tell me about your artwork. What do you want me to notice?
- What kinds of artwork do you enjoy the most?
- What materials do you like to work with?
- Do you have plans for something you would like to create?
- What changes do you see in your artwork this year?
- Where do you get your ideas? Do you know ahead of time what you are going to do, or does it change as you are doing it?
- Tell about a problem you had and how you solved it.
- How is your art changing, and what would you like to try next?

Drama: Suggested Activities

- Explain and demonstrate the following warm-up activities:
  Mirror Exercise (Be the leader for your parent, then change roles.)
  Mime Exercise (Together, mime making a bed or giving the dog a bath, planting potatoes, building a snowman, putting up a tent, stacking wood.)
- Show our class book, *The Emperor's New Clothes*. Tell which page you drew. What part did you have in the play?
- Show Dr. Seuss's book *The Sneetches*. Tell which part you had in the play we presented. Which was your favorite part? What did you do when the tone sounded?

51

Drama: Suggested Questions

- Did you enjoy performing in the *Wizard of Oz*? What part did you like the most?
- Have you been involved in making up any plays in the classroom?
- Do you like performing in front of a group?
- What do you enjoy doing most in your drama group with Heather?
- Tell about the role you have chosen in the play *Planet Nardo* and tell its significance for the community.

Physical Education: Suggested Activities

- Teach your favorite game.
- Use the balance beam, bounce a ball, skip across the room.
- Is there something you wish you could do better in gym?
- Show your guests what you like to do at gym time.
  Can you do something now that you couldn't do when you first came to school?
- Demonstrate two or three yoga poses (the dog, the cat, the cobra, the tree, the mountain).
  Use the balance beam (forward, backward, sideways)
  Skip rope.
  Bounce a ball.
- Show your parents how to play one of our tag games.
- Demonstrate what you have been learning in noon-hour jazz dance.
- If you took part in Mini-soccer on Thursdays at noon, demonstrate some of the skills you have learned.

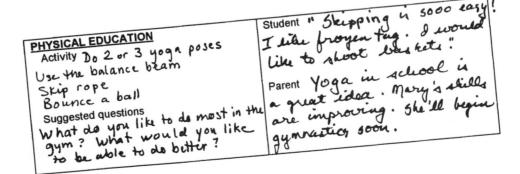

PHYSICAL EDUCATION
Activity Do 2 or 3 yoga poses
Use the balance beam
Skip rope
Bounce a ball
Suggested questions
What do you like to do most in the gym? What would you like to be able to do better?

Student "Skipping is sooo easy! I like frozen tag. I would like to shoot baskets."

Parent Yoga in school is a great idea. Mary's skills are improving. She'll begin gymnastics soon.

Physical Education: Suggested Questions

- What do you enjoy doing the most in the gym?
- What do you usually do outside during recess?
- Is there anything you like to be able to do better?
- Are you doing anything outside school time that is helping you keep fit?
- What can you do at school, in after-school programs (gymnastics, swimming, skating, ballet, soccer), or at home that you couldn't do before?
- Do you participate actively in all activities?
- Are you a good sport about winning and losing?
- Can you play hard without injuring yourself often?

Chloe and Michael take turns showing their skills on the balance beam.

Social and Emotional Development: Suggested Activities

- If I asked you to play a game with two friends in the class, whom would you choose? Why?
- What activity have you enjoyed the most during Buddy Time?
- What is your buddy's name? What do you like best about your buddy?
- What was your favorite Wonderful Wednesday project? [A block of time when primary students are put into mixed-age groups.]

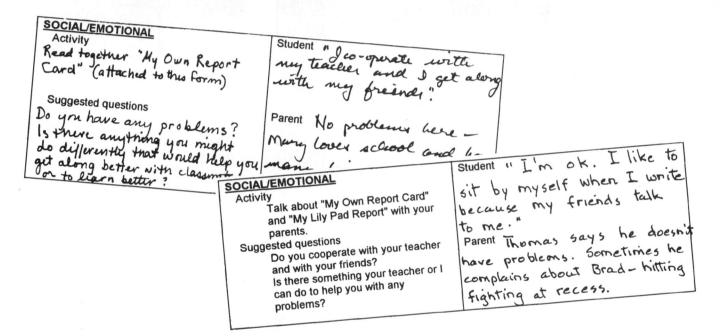

SOCIAL/EMOTIONAL

Activity
Read together "My Own Report Card" (attached to this form)

Suggested questions
Do you have any problems?
Is there anything you might do differently that would help you get along better with classmates or to learn better?

Student "I co-operate with my teacher and I get along with my friends."

Parent No problems here — Mary loves school and h...

SOCIAL/EMOTIONAL

Activity
Talk about "My Own Report Card" and "My Lily Pad Report" with your parents.

Suggested questions
Do you cooperate with your teacher and with your friends?
Is there something your teacher or I can do to help you with any problems?

Student "I'm ok. I like to sit by myself when I write because my friends talk to me."

Parent Thomas says he doesn't have problems. Sometimes he complains about Brad — hitting fighting at recess.

Social and Emotional Development: Suggested Questions

- Is there anything on My Own Report Card that you need to discuss together or with your teacher?
- Do you usually get to school on time, take home notices and newsletters, and return library books and forms?
- Do you use your time wisely in class?
- Has your behavior changed since September?
- Are you working to change anything about your behavior?

- Do you believe that your behavior helps you and others learn well?
- Do you get along well with your classmates in the classroom?
  At recess?
- When you have a problem with a friend, what strategies do you use to settle the conflict?

Satomi and her mom discuss her behavior at school.

Michael tells his mom some of the things he's learned about the Titanic.

Chapter 6

Other Teachers, Other Schools, Other Schedules

The three 1 1/2 hour conference blocks, with about eight families participating at each time, has worked well at our school. We organize our schedules so that we teachers enjoy a potluck or catered dinner together in the staff room between the afternoon and evening sessions. Of course, there is no one conference that is best for all schools; other teachers have established different schedules that work for them. On the next few pages I share the approaches of six different teachers. Use their ideas to help you design a schedule that suits your school community.

Larry

Larry, one of our own South Park teachers, schedules four student-led conference times during the year. His follows an open-house format: students can bring their parents to his classroom any time from 3 to 7 P.M. on four designated days spaced throughout the year. The days do not coincide with the rest of the classes' conference days. He doesn't ask families to sign up for certain times: The numbers always seem to work out.

Shelagh

Shelagh has the permission of her principal to hold conferences on certain school days, twice a year. Students do not attend classes on these days except during the hour they attend with their parents. She schedules four families each hour between 8 A.M. and 3:30 P.M., with a half-hour break for lunch.

Linda

Linda has tried two different schedules, both of which have been successful. In the first, students attend school until noon on a Wednesday, the teachers' professional day. (Students are usually dismissed at 1:45.) Conferences begin at 12:15 and last until about 5:30. About five families sign up for a series of one-hour periods. When she has not been able to close the classroom for a time during a normal day, she asks families to come before (8 to 9 A.M.) and after school (3 to 4 P.M., 4 to 5 P.M.). She has ten-minute three-way interviews with each family during these sessions. She admits that having to teach that day as well as conduct interviews is tiring, but she believes that the benefits outweigh the disadvantages.

She stresses that the preconference meeting for the parents is important. At that meeting she talks about the purpose of the student-led conferences and shows parents how to complete the Student Progress Report forms. Questions and concerns can be addressed at this time, as well.

Diane

Diane is a primary teacher who has organized student-led conferences at all primary grade levels. In the fall she invites each of her students' parents to the classroom for a morning in September or October (see invitation, Page 59). She thinks— and the parents agree— that it's interesting and informative for them to observe their child in the classroom for a morning or a full day. Diane gives them a sheet with suggestions about what to look for in the class (see page 60).

In the spring Diane sets up student-led conferences similar to the ones I hold. She asks families to sign up for sessions every 15 minutes beginning after school on a Wednesday, a short school day. She says that staggered starting times give her a chance to greet each family as they arrive. A sample of the Parents' Report she used one term is on page 61. Parents are asked to make comments about the different things their children have shown them and to decide on "two stars and a wish" for their child.

The families stay for about an hour. At the end of their tour they go to the multipurpose room to view a video of the class participating in gym, music, and drama activities.

Diane writes her reports two or three weeks after the conferences. She likes to refer to the parents' comments and address their major concerns.

Please Visit Our Classroom

Would you like to spend some time in our classroom to see what school is like for your child? I hope so. Please accept this invitation to visit our classroom for observation.

On the bottom of this page is a form to let me know when you will be visiting. Mornings are preferable, but if a morning visit isn't convenient for you, we can arrrange a time that is.

I look forward to spending this time with you, to answer any questions you may have about our classroom program, the goals we share for your child, and the progress your child is making. Please complete and return the form below so I can schedule and confirm your visit.

_____
Teacher's Signature

- Tear Here -

Mon. __   Tues. __   Wed. __   Thurs. __   Fri. __

Comment:
_____
_____
_____
_____
_____

_____   _____   _____
Child's Name   Parent's Signature   Phone

(Adapted from Diane Cowden and Alison Preece, *Young Writers in the Making*. Permission granted to duplicate.)

Your Comments and Observations

_____ _____ _____
    Child's Name   Parent's Name   Date

Welcome to Our Class!

Please use this form to share your thoughts:

The way your child interacted with other children: _____
_____
_____

Your child's attitude toward learning: _____
_____
_____

Your child's participation during whole-class group time:
_____
_____

Your child's attitude toward and involvement with writing:
_____
_____

Your child's feeling toward books: _____
_____
_____

Something that surprised you about the way we learn in this classroom:
_____
_____

Something special about the progress your child is making:
_____
_____

     We hope you will share your thoughts with your child, and we look forward to your next visit.

(Adapted from Diane Cowden and Alison Preece, *Young Writers in the Making*. Permission granted to duplicate.)

Parents' Report
Please Share Your Comments

Name: _____

Date: _____

Center	✓	Comments
1. Weather Mural		
2. China		
3. Writing: -journal -writing folder -printing		
4.. Home is Best: literature		
5. Mathematics		
6. Big Buddies		
7. Reader's Theater		
8. Sheep Farm Display		
9. Science		
10. Computer		

Two Stars _____

One Wish _____

Any further comments or suggestions? _____
_____

(Adapted from Diane Cowden and Alison Preece, *Young Writers in the Making.*)

Create a form like this to reflect your particular conference centers.

Wendy

Wendy also asks parents to "give two stars and a wish" for their child. Her form explains: "The two stars tell two things (skills, knowledge, attitude) that show growth in your child's development and how you know that they have grown. The wish tells me what you hope for your child or what you would like your child to develop or focus on next term." I added this to my own latest conference form, and I like the results.

The letter she sends home explains student-led conferences to parents:

Dear Parents,

Here is some important information about the upcoming reporting period. After your child's report card comes home on March 31, you will be invited to attend student-led conferences. The conferences will take place on Wednesday, April 5. Please fill out the bottom of the form for the time that best suits your family.

Students will have an opportunity to show you what they have been doing at school. They will explain classroom routines, share their work and demonstrate their skills.

Parents will have an opportunity to watch their child working in many different areas. There is an opportunity to encourage your child by giving positive, accepting feedback, and to strengthen their self-esteem by seeing them in a position of responsibility. You will have time to ask questions and discover new insights into their learning.

Teachers will move around the room and have an opportunity to meet with each child and his or her family. There will be seven or eight families working through the stations at one time.

It would be very disappointing for your child if no one can attend. Please try to make yourselves available for this conference. If it is not possible, an alternative is to ask a grandparent or another relative to take your place.

This can be a very special time for you and your child. Please make arrangements for other siblings to be looked after so that nothing will distract you from this special sharing together.

Please indicate the times you are available to come to school with your child for the Student-Led Conferences on Wednesday, April 5.

2:00–2:45 _____
3:00–3:45 _____
4:00–4:45 _____

5:00–5:45 _____
6:00–6:45 _____

Thank you.

Anne

In Anne's class, each child prepares a folder of work to show his or her parents. Into each folder Anne tucks a special note of appreciation written especially for that child. This note will be a surprise for both student and parents during the conference. This folder is put at one of the centers. The other centers consist of hands-on activities.

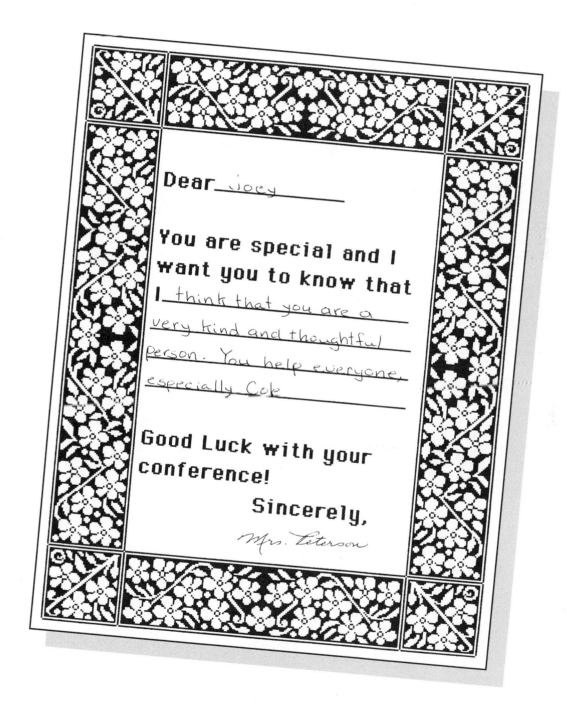

Dear Joey

You are special and I want you to know that I think that you are a very kind and thoughtful person. You help everyone, especially Cole

Good Luck with your conference!

Sincerely,

Mrs. Peterson

Chapter 7

Reports and Comments on Conferences

We have always asked the parents attending the conferences to write remarks—a word or two, a phrase, a short sentence—on the program forms. After the first conferences, we asked them to write a direct quote from their child as well. It occurred to us primary teachers that we might write our own remarks about each student here, too.

Could this take the place of the standard report card? Why not? It would be a three-way report card, with all of the people concerned taking part, including the student. Since Liz Hamblett, our principal at the time, would also be making a short comment, four people would be involved. Fortunately, South Park is a place where we are encouraged to try things that we believe would benefit our students. Liz told us to go ahead and try it.

The first three-way report card was simply an expanded student-led conference program form. In the comment box on the right we wrote Student, Parent, and Teacher. We included many more Suggested Questions for parents to ask in each center. We invited parents to write direct quotes from their child for the Student part and to make their own brief comments in the Parent section. At the end of the report I ask parents to answer, "Do you have any questions about any area of your child's development?"

We have tried different approaches to the completion of these reports over the years. Sometimes we've written our own comments after the conferences. I like this because I can answer questions parents have asked about different academic or social curricular areas and respond to their comments. You wil find sample three-way report cards on pages 66 through 69.

South Park School
Victoria, B.C.

Early Primary Class
Teacher: Linda Picciotto

STUDENT PROGRESS REPORT
by
Student-Teacher-Parent
November, 1995

Student's name: **Brad Codell** Age: **6** years **4** months

INTELLECTUAL DEVELOPMENT

My goal is to provide a program that allows all children, regardless of their developmental levels, the chance to achieve success and continue to grow and to feel good about themselves as people and as learners.

--daily roll call and "calendar jobs", incorporating math, language skills, French

--almost daily writing and reading "the news" to develop a complete range of skills including phonics and other reading and writing techniques

--almost daily Writing Workshop to allow students to practice their writing skills at their own levels

--daily reading time and story time

--sharing of their own reading and writing to hear comments and encouragement from me, other adults, and their peers

--problem solving and mathematical concepts discussed and practiced in meaningful contexts where possible. We also are working on printing numerals properly. Our pumpkins provided us with a chance to compare, weigh, measure, and count!

--frequent discussions to develop thinking skills, language, knowledge

--science--beaver study, micro-biology studies arranged by Fran Nano (professor at UVIC), which included studying cultures grown from clean and dirty hands and making yogurt, and mini-studies inspired by things contributed by students and by articles and books read together

--daily Activity Time to allow children to develop academic and social skills and to pursue their own interests

Reading

Read to your parents the material you have chosen.

Possible questions:

What can you read now that you couldn't before?

Which books do you look at or read during reading time?

What can you do to try to read words you don't know right away?

What is helping you learn to read (something you do at home? at school? by yourself? with a friend, parent or teacher?

How do you feel about reading?

Is there something you would like us to help you with at home?

Student "I like the orange Get Ready books. When I don't know a word I sound it out, skip it or ask someone."

Parent We notice that Brad is taking more chances and guesses sometimes when he doesn't know the word. We have fun reading together.

Teacher I notice that Brad is making progress in his reading, too. He can read sentences on the level of our "morning news" quite fluently, even without picture clues. I'm sure his reading at home has helped him gain confidence. Keep it up!

Six-year-old Brad shares a reading strategy he uses.

66

Writing

Look at your Duo-tang collection of weekly writing samples with your parents. You can also show any other writing samples you have selected.

Suggested questions:

What can you do now in writing that you couldn't in September?

What skills are you working on now?

What do you like best about Writing Workshop?

What is helping you learn to write? (something at home? at school?)

Is there anything you would like us to help you with at home? (printing practice?)

Student "I write well now. I write larger sentences. I print neater."

Parent Brad prefers to memorize full words. He knows some word endings like "ing". He's trying to remember to separate his words.

Teacher Brad's writing ability has increased considerably. He uses many more "real sounds", he separates his words, and he uses standard spelling for many of the short, frequently-used words (the, of, on, then...) When inspired he can write long, well-constructed sentences. See his discription of Toby's experiment — what an improvement over his first "science write-up" attempt! [Toby pot a GLaSovr a kndl...]

Mathematics

10
+ 10
= 20

At the math centre, weigh the two pumpkins. Measure the circumference of one of them. Count the seeds in the dish by first grouping them in 10s.

Suggested questions:

What can you do with numbers that you couldn't do last year?

What more would you like to learn about mathematics? Which kind of activities do you enjoy the most? (working with higher numbers, telling time, graphing, making and noticing patterns, measuring, weighing, estimating, problem solving....)

Is there something you would like us to help you with at home?

Student "I like math. I like to weigh things and count high. I can read big numbers."

Parent Math was the first table Brad went to. He counted, weighed and measured with ease. He enjoys card games, dice games and Monopoly at home and has made out his first bank draft.

Teacher

Brad has a strength in math. He participates well in problem-solving and is helpful to others when they have difficulty understanding. Maybe he could bring in a bank deposit slip to show us: money is always inspiring!

Science

1. Using our murals as a guide, tell what you know now about beavers.

2. Go down to the multi-purpose room together. Take your science book. Tell about what you did and show the pages in your book.

Suggested questions:

What did you learn that you did not know before about the beaver?

Which part of your studies about micro-biology did you find the most interesting?

Do you enjoy learning about things like animals, plants, magnets, chemistry, rocks, and electricity? What would you like to learn about this year?

Student "I liked making yogurt. It was fun building the beaver lodge."

Parent Brad learned a lot about beavers. He was proud of the mural. I'm happy to see him excited about science.

Teacher

He is one of our really keen students in science. He asks good questions and makes interesting observations. He has contributed a lot to our discussions. He has good general knowledge.

Brad's parents' comments show how much they've learned about their son's development.

AESTHETIC AND ARTISTIC DEVELOPMENT

Students have been singing in class and have attended music lessons with Christine twice a week. Many have chosen to join the Primary Choir.

They have completed many works of art in the classroom, most of their own choosing during Writing Workshop time and Activity Time. We have completed several directed projects, as well, both 2- and 3-dimensional, that were designed to give students new experiences with techniques and subject matter. They worked in groups to complete murals about beaver life. Students have had a variety of art experiences based on the work of different illustrators in our Wonderful Wednesday sessions. In my class they study the work of Ted Harrison.

ART	
Go through your art portfolio together.	**Student** "I'm using more colour now. I like the lion picture I did with oil pastels."
Suggested questions:	**Parent** I'm glad to see him drawing a variety of things and using different materials. I was tired of Ninja turtles! I like his art work.
What do you want me to notice about your art work? What kinds of art work do you enjoy the most? What materials do you like to work with? Do you have plans for something you would like to create? What changes do you see in your art work this year?	**Teacher** Brad likes to draw detailed pictures that are full of action. He can tell a good story with his art. I'm happy to see him use color now, too. Didn't he do a wonderful job with the corn stalk he painted?

MUSIC	
Visit Christine's music centre.	**Student** "I am learning to beat. I like to sing the Oliver songs."
Suggested questions:	**Parent** Continues to enjoy music and likes to share new songs with us. He is still shy about singing in front of others.
What have you been learning in music class? Why did you choose (or not choose) to be in the Primary Choir? Do you have a favourite song?	**Teacher** I'm glad he shares his singing at home. I've noticed that he's a little self-conscious about singing with the group, but he often joins in. He can follow his part in a round.

Brad's parents share important insights into Brad's learning at home.

68

PHYSICAL DEVELOPMENT

Students join me in daily exercises in the classroom in increase their flexibility and to stretch their legs after sitting on the carpet. We have two gym periods a week for tag games, work with the parachute, free play with balls, hoops, bean bags, and skipping ropes. We enjoy frequent outings to the playground and to Beacon Hill Park.

Demonstrate in the gym:

Two or three yoga poses (the dog, the cat, the cobra, the tree, the mountain...)

Use the balance beam (forwards and backwards)

Show three different ways you can use the scooter boards.

Bounce a ball with both hands and then with each hand alone.

Suggested questions:

What can you do now at school, in after school programs (gymnastics, swimming, skating, ballet.....) or at home that you couldn't before?

What would you like to be able to do better?

What are your favourite activities in the gym?

Student "I can swim better and skate better. I like gymnastics. I want to play basketball."

Parent I'm glad Brad enjoys gym time. He's going to start baseball in April.

Teacher

Brad loves to go to the gym. He shoots beanbags at the hoop with great enthusiasm and joins actively in all other games. He is well coordinated – he's even learned to skip!

EMOTIONAL AND SOCIAL DEVELOPMENT
DEVELOPMENT OF SOCIAL RESPONSIBILITY

I have been noting how students listen to and participate in class discussions, lessons, and activities. I have been looking for evidence of active involvement with classmates and actions and comments that indicate development of empathy and self esteem. I have been watching to see how children's actions are helping to create a "community of learners".

With your parent(s), look at "My Own Report Card" and the "Lily Pad Report"

Suggested questions:

Has your behavior changed since September?

Are you working to change anything about your behavior?

Do you believe that your behavior helps you and others to learn well at school?

Do you get along well with your classmates?

Can you solve problems by talking instead of hurting?

Student "I'm good. I always listen and cooperate. I'm nice to everyone and I share."

Parent Brad is certainly full of fun. I'm proud of his growing ability to be part of a group.

Teacher I enjoy having Brad in my class. He has a nice sense of humor – enjoys a funny story, laughs at my jokes, makes up some of his own! He's participating better in class discussions. He is happier speaking to a small group. He is always cooperative and helpful. He always has ideas for interesting activities during activity time. He likes to build things with friends.

Brad celebrates his ability to get along with others.

Sometimes we have written comments before the conferences. Some parents tell me they like this system because it gives them something more concrete to look for at the conference.

Those of us who like to use the word processor found it difficult to complete the form with our comments separated into the different curricular areas, so for the next report we left spaces for only the parents' and students' comments, and made our own remarks in paragraph form at the end. We're still working on ways to shorten the time we have to spend writing report cards. We have some ideas we're going to try.

The Form Evolves

First, the form was just a single letter-size piece of paper, then that became a two-page booklet. After that it was a two-page legal-size booklet.

Viv, our new kindergarten teacher, suggested turning the legal-size paper sideways and creating a two-page, four-sided booklet. We liked the idea.

I started attaching samples of the students' work to the forms (writing from the beginning of the term and writing from term's end, samples of My Best Printing, a favorite drawing, and the different Self-Evaluation forms we asked them to complete—see my book *Evaluation: A Team Effort* for sample forms). Then I thought that by adding pages to the booklet we could include some of the self-evaluation forms or work samples as part of the report itself, instead of stapling extra papers at the back. It would look neater and the students' work would somehow seem more important if it were part of the official document. I increased the number of pages in the little booklet to accommodate the new information.

At one point we began asking students to prepare cover pages and to make little black-ink drawings throughout the report card to illustrate the different areas. They add charm to the document, make it personal, and help the students become familiar with the centers.

Other Changes

We decided to put our Curriculum Overviews directly onto the forms to give parents a better idea of our programs and the activities their children had participated in at school. We thought the inclusion of overviews would decrease the amount of writing we'd have to do on each report, as well: We wouldn't have to repeat on each one what we'd taught or what things we were looking for as we assessed our students. The overviews in each area would change somewhat from term to term but most would remain the same. Once typed, they would simply be modified for the next form. We hoped this would save time, and we were right.

I suggest that you hold your first student-led conferences separate from reporting, although they could be held roughly at the same time or in place of parent-teacher interviews. Once the parents and teachers have become used to the format, reporting can be added more easily.

I hope that you will try student-led conferences. I certainly hope that you find them so wonderful that you will continue to use them as part of your classroom program. I hope that you will find, as I have, that parents, students, and teachers benefit greatly from this shared experience.

Bibliography
Recommended Reading

Baskwill, J. *Parents and Teachers: Partners in Learning*. Richmond Hill, ON: Scholastic Canada Ltd., 1989.

Davies, Anne, C. Cameron, C. Politano, and K. Gregory. *Together Is Better: Collaboration, Assessment, Evaluation, and Reporting*. Winnepeg, MB: Peguis Publishers Limited, 1992.

Fisher, Bobbi. *Thinking and Learning Together: Curriculum and Community in a Primary Classroom*. Portsmouth, NH: Heinemann, 1995.

Forester, Anne D. and Margaret Reinhard. *The Learners' Way*. Winnipeg, MB: Peguis Publishers Limited, 1989.

Forester, Anne D. and Margaret Reinhard. *On the Move*. Winnipeg, MB: Peguis Publishers Limited, 1991.

Forester, Anne D. and Margaret Reinhard. *The Teacher's Way*. Winnipeg, MB: Peguis Publishers Limited, 1994.

Harsle, J., V. Woodward and C. Burke. *Language Stories and Literacy Lessons*. Portsmouth, NH: Heinemann, 1984.

Hill, Bonnie Campbell, and Cynthia Ruptic. *Practical Aspects of Authentic Assessment: Putting the Pieces Together*. Norwood, MA: Christopher-Gordon Publishers, Inc., 1994.

Little, Nancy and John Allan. *Student-Led Teacher-Parent Conferences*. Toronto, ON: Lugus Publications, 1988.

Peetoom, Adrian. *Professional Reflections and Connections*. Richmond Hill, ON: Scholastic Canada Ltd., 1992.

Picciotto, Linda Pierce. *Evaluation: A Team Effort*. Richmond Hill, ON: Scholastic Canada Ltd., 1992.

Picciotto, Linda Pierce. *Learning Together: A Whole Year in a Primary Classroom* (Canadian title), *Managing an Integrated Language Arts Classroom* (U.S. title), 1993, 1995.

Preece, Alison, and Diane Cowden. *Young Writers in the Making: Sharing the Process with Parents*. Portsmouth, NH: Heinemann, 1993.

Appendix
Blank Sample Forms

Letter to Parents from Teacher (Form 1)
This letter to parents gives an overview of student-led conferences. Make copies and send home.

Letter to Parents from Student (Form 2)
This letter from the child to the parents reminds moms and dads about the conferences. Make copies and send home.

Student-Led Conference Form (Form 3a-3c)
This three-page form consists of a cover page and two conference pages. Ask students to complete the cover page by drawing a picture and writing a message on the lines. Ask students to decorate the form by making appropriate drawings in the margins with ball-point pens, crayons, or colored pencils.

Student/Teacher/Parent Report (Form 4a-4e)
In the space under the major headings write your Curriculum Overview, and activities and suggested questions for each center. (See pages 37 through 58 of this book for ideas.) You may turn this form into a booklet.

(For examples of how one of my students, his parents, and I completed these forms, see pages 66 through 69.)

Feedback from Parents (Form 5a-5b) (long)
Make copies, then distribute to parents.

Feedback from Parents (Form 6) (short)
Make copies, then distribute to parents.

Feedback from Students (Form 7)
Make copies, then distribute to students.

It's Conference Time!

Date _____

Dear Parents,

Student-led conferences will be held soon in our classroom. Your child is ready to show you what he or she is learning at school and to tell you about plans for the next term.

Your child will take you to a number of different centers in the classroom, where he or she will show you work completed or demonstrate skills. You will have an opportunity to write brief comments and observations and to jot down things your child says about the different subjects. I have allowed one and a half hours for each session, but you do not have to stay the entire time—or you may stay longer.

Since you will want to focus your attention on your child in my class, please do not bring along his or her siblings. If you cannot attend during any of the time slots, we can make another appointment, or a grandparent, aunt or uncle, or family friend might attend instead.

There will be about eight other families in the room at the same time, visiting the centers in different order. I will circulate and join your family conference from time to time, but it is your child who will be in charge. At the end of the session, your child will serve refreshments.

If you wish to schedule an appointment to speak privately with me after the conference, please let me know and I'll be happy to meet with you.

The blocks of time available for the student-led conferences are:

_____   _____   _____   _____

Please sign up on the sheet outside my room or send a note with your child telling which time is best for you.

I look forward to seeing you then.

Sincerely,

_____

Your Conference Date

Date _____

Dear _____,

Please remember to come to my student-led
conference!

It is on _____

at _____ o'clock.

I will show you around the classroom and tell
you what I am learning at school.

My teacher, _____,

is looking forward to seeing you, too.

Love,

_____

Name: _____ **Age:** _____

```
┌─────────────────────────────────────────┐
│                                         │
│                                         │
│                                         │
│                                         │
│                                         │
│                                         │
│                                         │
│                                         │
│                                         │
└─────────────────────────────────────────┘
```

_____

_____

_____

Dear Parents,

Welcome to my student-led conference! We may go to the different learning centers in any order. I'm going to show you what I am learning in school.

Love,

_____

Dear Parents,

For each center, please print a quote from your child in the Comments sections of the form. You may make your own short comment at the same time or write it at home later. Please be sure to return the form as soon as possible, for it is part of our three-way report.

Enjoy your conference!

Sincerely,
Your child's teacher

STUDENT-LED CONFERENCE

Student_____ Parent(s)_____ Date_____

CENTERS	COMMENTS
READING Activity Suggested questions	Student Parent
WRITING Activity Suggested questions	Student Parent
MATH Activity Suggested questions	Student Parent
SCIENCE/SOCIAL STUDIES Activity Suggested questions	Student Parent

PHYSICAL EDUCATION Activity	Student
Suggested questions	Parent
MUSIC Activity	Student
Suggested questions	Parent
ART Activity	Student
Suggested questions	Parent
SOCIAL/EMOTIONAL Activity	Student
Suggested questions	Parent
Activity	Student
Suggested questions	Parent

Now, enjoy a snack together at the refreshment table!

Student _____ Age: Years _____ Months _____

Grade _____ School _____

Teacher _____ Date_____

Student Progress Report
by
Student-Teacher-Parent

COGNITIVE DEVELOPMENT

_____
_____
_____
_____
_____
_____
_____
_____
_____
_____
_____

READING Activity	COMMENTS Student
	Parent
Suggested questions	Teacher

WRITING	COMMENTS
Activity	Student
	Parent
Suggested questions	Teacher

MATHEMATICS	COMMENTS
Activity	Student
	Parent
Suggested questions	Teacher

SCIENCE/SOCIAL STUDIES	COMMENTS
Activity	Student
	Parent
Suggested questions	Teacher

AESTHETIC AND ARTISTIC DEVELOPMENT

ART	COMMENTS
Activity	Student
	Parent
Suggested questions	Teacher

MUSIC	COMMENTS
Activity	Student
	Parent
Suggested questions	Teacher

DRAMA	COMMENTS
Activity	Student
	Parent
Suggested questions	Teacher

(Form 4c)

PHYSICAL DEVELOPMENT

PHYSICAL EDUCATION Activity	COMMENTS Student
	Parent
Suggested questions	Teacher

EMOTIONAL AND SOCIAL DEVELOPMENT

EMOTIONAL/SOCIAL Activity	COMMENTS Student
	Parent
Suggested questions	Teacher

Do you have any questions about your child's progress in any area?

_____

_____

_____

_____

_____

Principal's Comments

_____

_____

_____

_____

_____

_____

Signatures:

Student _____   Parent _____

Teacher _____   Principal _____

Date _____

Dear Parents,

Recently, you and your child participated in student-led conferences. Would you please take a few moments to answer the following questions.

Your comments will help us plan our next conferences so that they will be as enjoyable and meaningful as possible for our families.

Thank you.

1. Did the activities help you learn what you wanted to know about your child's progress and attitudes toward learning and school?

_____

_____

_____

2. Did the conferences (in addition to my written report card) inform you adequately about your child's progress without a separate parent-teacher conference?

_____

_____

_____

3. What were the benefits of student-led conferences for your child?

_____

_____

_____

4. What were the benefits of student-led conferences for you, the adult(s) (or custodians)?

_____

_____

_____

5. Was the conference the right length?

_____

_____

_____

6. Which centers were particularly interesting or instructive for you or your child?

_____

_____

_____

7. Were there any centers or activities that took too long?

_____

_____

_____

8. Were there any centers or activities you would like to see added, changed, or omitted?

_____

_____

_____

9. If this was your first conference, were you given enough information beforehand about what to expect? If not, what would have been helpful?

_____

_____

_____

10. Do you have anything else to add? Are there any comments your child made before, during, or after the conferences that you would like to share with us?

_____

_____

_____

Student _____   Parent _____

Student _____ **Grade** _____ **Parent** _____

Dear Parent,

Would you please take a few moments to answer the following questions. Your responses will help me when I plan next term's conferences. Thank you.

1. Please tell me what you liked about the student-led conferences.

_____

_____

_____

2. What might be added or changed to make them more successful, meaningful, or enjoyable for you or your child?

_____

_____

_____

3. Were you able to notice anything about your child's attitudes toward school and learning that you might not have seen without the conferences? Please explain.

_____

_____

_____

4. Anything else?

_____

_____

_____

Thank you.

My name is

_____ •

```




                    (Here I am at my student-led conference.)

```

Our student-led conferences were held this week.

Mine was on _____ .

My _____ came to my conference.

My favorite center was _____ .

One thing my _____ said was _____

_____

I thought _____

_____ .

Notes